Minister Allen does a masterful job in revealing the revelation that we are much more than our experiences. He helps us to see that regardless of our mistakes, shortcomings, hurt, pain, and rejections, God esteems us as precious and valuable to Him. A value we cannot see until we bring our shortcomings, deficiencies, experiences, and limitations to Him, in exchange for His love, wholeness, and acceptance. It is only then that we can discover our true identity, value, and purpose in life. *I Am More Than My Experiences* is a must-read to discover how to be released into who God created you to be!

Pastor Cynthia Marshall
Victory Christian Ministries International-DC

In this book, Allen Forbes encourages the reader to know and love God, recognizing that it is through this process that we are able to truly know and love ourselves. This all-encompassing knowing and unconditional love includes forgiving ourselves of mistakes, poor decisions, and bad experiences of the past, and embracing who we are in God's sight. With brevity, he shares engaging stories to set the stage for thought-provoking comments, biblical principles, words of encouragement, recommendations for moving forward, and chapter-ending points to ponder.

He carefully intermingles bible stories, lessons learned, and insights that serve as the basis for reflection, introspection, and direction. Forbes propels us forward with tools to succeed, as he reminds the reader (women in particular) that they (I and we) are not defined by any act or experiences, but are indeed *so much more."*

Dr. Genevieve Floyd

This latest impartation by Minister Allen Forbes, *I Am More Than My Experiences,* gently challenges and guides us to take a hard look at the experiences that shape our current self-image, to qualify them, and to take specific actions to validate them in light of our pursuit of God. Shared with the heart of a learned servant, this book will encourage women (and men) to be real with themselves about where they are in life, and to courageously take the required steps for growth.
Ivy Coleman
The Message Ministry International

My first thoughts after completing the book were that I have to read it again to make sure I got it all, and a desire to tell everyone I know that they have to buy this book! The book is very timely considering the impact of the pandemic and political unrest. Depending on how we are affected by those distractions, they can change who we are and what we will become.

The book will be profound and transformational for not only women, but for all who will read it. Even with strong spiritual beliefs, the book raised awareness that one needs to work on maintaining their spiritual identity and purpose, especially now. I had previously read or heard the stories of the Bible that were referenced in the book, after reading *I Am More Than My Experiences,* I now have a new perspective of them. What a blessing it was!
Dr. Brenda Bullock

Have you ever asked yourself: Who am I? What's my life assignment? *I Am More Than My Experiences* is a book that shifts your view from the rear-view mirror to the windshield. The book is designed for us women to continue forging progressively by living beyond feelings and overcoming fear and insecurities, to discovering our true identity. Imagine discovering the abundant blessings and deep satisfaction that you were created for. Imagine understanding that you are graced to dismantle self-defeating habits and rise to unlock new realms of meaningful living.

We are in a time where women are carrying more influence than in any other generation; women are shattering glass ceilings and fearlessly moving forward with purpose without any limits into new paths in the world. This book states it brilliantly, that "God is power and there is nothing greater than His force." Self-reflection is needed to have the right perception and for the right perspective. Woman, be intentional! You have been uniquely and wonderfully crafted by God to make it. This book highlights **nine** essential truths about identity. Don't wait; you are just a step away from unlocking your identity. Begin your practical life-changing exciting journey of self-reflection to find fulfillment with ease.

Pastor OluBunmi Olarinde
RCCG- Mercy Seat Chapel

I Am More Than My Experiences

A Woman's Transformational Journey
To Discovering Her True Identity

Allen Forbes

I Am More Than My Experiences
Copyright © 2021 by Allen Forbes
ISBN 978-0-9977123-4-6

Unless otherwise indicated, all scripture quotations are taken from the King James Version of the Bible.

Printed in the United States of America. All rights reserved under international copyright law. Contents and/or cover may not be reproduced in whole or part without the express written consent of the publisher.

Published by Allen Forbes
P.O. Box 305
Germantown, MD 20875

Library of Congress Control Number: 2020919740

Cover design by Alloy Consulting Group LLC

Your experiences do not have to define who you are!

Table of Contents

Acknowledgements 1
Foreword 3
Introduction 5
Chapter One 9
Chapter Two 23
Chapter Three 33
Chapter Four 43
Chapter Five 51
Chapter Six 59
The Conclusion 67
About the Author 73
Other Books 75

Acknowledgements

I'd like to say thank you:
To the many friends, professional editors and readers of my manuscript who proofed, edited and provided thoughtful, wise and fearless feedback. I'm truly blessed and honored that I know you! Specifically, to –

Dr. Carla McNeal for your editing expertise and advice.

Lloyda, my wife, friend, and proofreader/advisor. You are an inspiration, strength and support. Your encouragement never goes without notice.

Finally, to all of the wonderful women out there who are struggling to find themselves as well as those who will not allow their experiences to define them - I say

Thank you all!

Foreword

I Am More Than My Experiences will capture and keep your attention. Allen Forbes has a heart to see people become who they were meant to be and you will feel his heart through the nuggets that he imparts. At the very beginning of the book, Allen writes: "Instead of repeating your past, reset your future." This statement is incredibly salient and much needed for all of us. The author is being used by God to challenge people to develop a powerful mindset and determination to overcome. The insight shared in *I Am More Than My Experiences* provokes us to walk under the governing of God's Holy Spirit and not the flesh.

His perspective on how women can move beyond their past is eye-opening. When a woman looks to exchange her issues by receiving the grace of God, she moves from being a woman with an issue to being a daughter. This book outlines that progression. We often employ the natural by exhausting all of our resources, and forgo an encounter with the Lord that could transform our lives. Many settle for a lowly position because of their past experiences. This book encourages the reader to reach for more. To believe for the promises that God has for us while transcending beyond what we can see naturally.

We recommend that you make time to read this book. Your identity will develop beyond your past as you walk in the fullness of God's plans for you. Be blessed as you enjoy what the Lord will show you through *I Am More Than My Experiences.*

Pastors David and Tracy Whittington
Redemption House Life Center

Introduction

It is unfortunate when a woman is not truly seen. She may often only be viewed as a mom, sister, lover, girlfriend, or wife. Her identity can become masked by her title, career, roles, the expectations placed on her, and the customs of the day. Too often when her true identity is not seen by others, it is also hidden from her, as well.

Why is her value often looked at as less than rather than more than? Could this misplaced value be placed on her because others fear her true potential? Does her success, power, and independence intimidate those around her who have low self-esteem? The only thing worse than others not seeing her value, is when she cannot see it herself.

My daughter went out one day with some friends and while she was out, she dropped her iPhone. The screen cracked and she cried when it happened. I looked online to see what the cost was to fix the iPhone and shared that information with her. She decided that the cost was too much for her and reasoned that the phone still functioned with a cracked screen. I even offered to give her half the money to fix it, but she still did not fix it. She continued to use the phone for months with the screen completely shattered. She got used to seeing pictures of people and even herself broken and shattered.

After many talks with her, I decided to get her screen replaced. We got the phone fixed. She picked up the phone and said, "My phone looks like new." The screen was clear of all cracks and flaws. The first thing she did was take a selfie and she was able to see how beautiful she looked. We can get used to seeing things through a dim distorted glass or a broken lens. If this goes on for too long, we can somehow think that's the way things are supposed to be. Having a shattered lens and view of ourselves can give us a warped and broken perspective. It will be hard to receive new beautiful things when you don't believe you are worthy of them. Doubting yourself can haunt you and make you feel less than when you are more than.

Breaking a mindset is never easy. Real change takes commitment and work. Before you can make progress, your previous limits have to be removed. To remove the boundaries, you will need to be honest with yourself and unafraid to explore the issues that could be holding you back. This will aid you in seeing and believing that you are worthy of the next level.

Your life should be lived from the inside out. You were not meant to have external circumstances alter your course. Some of the experiences that you have gone through may have been horrific. I am sorry that you had to endure such things, but don't allow a horrible thing to stop you from living the marvelous life that God has for you. Instead of repeating your past, reset your future by bringing to light your true identity. Break out from the invisible limits that have been placed on you by your past and explore the new possibilities of your future!

Let the world see your true beauty, worth, and purpose—your identity!

See yourself. Agree with yourself. Be yourself!

Chapter One

Repeat

When I was in my twenties, I managed an electrical project at a commercial building in Washington, D.C. This was a rather large project and I had about 20 people reporting to me on a daily basis. I was very familiar with the dynamics of having that many team members and the challenges and attitudes that the workers could present. On this project, I needed more help and asked my boss for more manpower so that we could meet the customer's deadlines. That Thursday, he sent me a gentleman named Brian. Brian was an African-American apprentice with a few months' experience. He was a good worker and wanted to make sure that he did the job right. After working with him for a few days, he shared with me that he had been incarcerated for 7 years and had been out for the last 6 months or so. He was happy to be working because his wife was expecting. I had worked with other people who were previously incarcerated before, but Brian seemed to talk much more to me about his prison life than anyone else I had encountered. He often shared about the Muslims, the Black and Hispanic gangs, and the Aryan Nation. This did not bother me at all because he was still working hard and doing his job.

About ten days later, my boss sent me another gentleman named Juan. Juan was Latino and he was a licensed journeyman electrician. Juan was from New York City like me, and he was efficient and reliable. Juan also had tattoos all over his body; he was completely covered with them. After a few weeks, I gave Juan the task of installing some 4-inch electrical pipe in the basement of the building. I gave him the task in the morning and sent Brian with him as his helper. In less than 15 minutes, Brian came back to me telling me that he could not work with Juan. Brian explained to me that Juan knew he was previously incarcerated, so he was talking down to him. Brian was seriously frustrated and was telling me that I needed to talk with Juan before things got out of hand.

I went down to the basement and asked Juan what was going on. Juan mentioned that Brian wasn't listening to him but that everything was okay. I told Brian to take a 10-minute break and then go back and help Juan finish installing the pipe. I explained to Brian that they were not in prison anymore and to just work together on the task. He calmed down and was able to go back and work with Juan. I knew enough that I should be nearby so that I could watch the situation. About an hour later, I heard the sound of metal hitting the floor. I went to see what was going on and there was Brian hollering at Juan and threatening him. Juan was just ignoring him and installing the pipe. I took Brian outside for a breather and talked him down. I didn't want to fire him because I knew he deserved a chance, plus he had a baby on the way. After he calmed down, I sent him to go help someone else and I gave Juan another helper. Juan worked well with everyone else and I did not have any more problems with him.

I knew that it was a bad idea to put the two of them together again so I kept them separate. Brian still complained about Juan and the looks that he was getting from him. I tolerated some of the complaining because I wanted to meet our project deadlines. One day I was in the elevator and I got off on the mezzanine level. As I walked by the security desk, the security guard explained to me that one of my guys had threatened him. I asked him what happened and he said, "This guy just walked in and got into the elevator to go down to the basement without signing in." He stated that he went over to the elevator and told him he had to get off of the elevator and come over to the security desk and get a badge. He then said in a fearful voice that the individual (described as Brian) threatened him. Apparently, Brian said, "You better never talk to me like that again or I am going to hurt you."

I immediately went down to the basement and asked Brian to come with me outside. I asked him about the incident to hear his side of the story. He basically said that the security guard was hollering at him and disrespecting him. He said, "I told him that if he did that again, I was going to hurt him." I thought to myself, "*We have to work in this building, which is a public place, and if this guy is a time bomb, I will have to let him go.*" Giving him one more chance I said, "Brian, if you get in the elevator and some guy says something to you that is disrespectful what are you going to do?" Without hesitation he responded, "I am going to kick his ____. I am not going to allow anyone at any time to disrespect me." I immediately responded, "I wish you the best but I have to let you go." He said, "Allen, why man? Is it Juan? Is it because he is from New York and you guys have a New York thing? Why are you doing this to me? You can't be serious!" For me, it was not a hard decision to make because I had to look out for the welfare of the team and the people on site. I felt bad for Brian because although he was free from jail, he really wasn't. He still identified with his past experience more than the reality of the fact that he was free. He was no longer in a physical prison but a psychological one. His previous environment led him to a mindset where his actions became evident that he was still living in his past experiences.

Many of us can relate to this story to some degree or another. Something in our past has been a weight in our present. Women, especially, have had to bear so many things from past hurts, dysfunctional relationships, and unpleasant experiences. This is why knowing your true identity is so powerful and significant. Knowing who you really are will help you get beyond your past. Understanding your identity is crucial if you desire to advance and be your most authentic self.

What is identity?

Identity is the state or fact of remaining the same. It is the character, condition, qualities and beliefs that distinguish a person or thing. The English word "identity" comes from the Latin word *identitās,* which means repeatedly, again and again. A person's psychological identity relates to self-image or a mental picture of oneself. It becomes what a person sees over and over again. When a person sees his or her past over and over again, his or her identity and perspective are developed.

A person's identity consists of three things: **belief system, personality,** and **DNA**. A person's belief system is made up internally of values, principles, and convictions. Personality has to do with your character, traits, and behavior. DNA has to do with a person's uniqueness or his or her genetic code or fingerprint. This is the mark that a person leaves behind to show evidence of existence. Therefore, *identity is an internal conviction that leads to a behavior that affirms existence.*

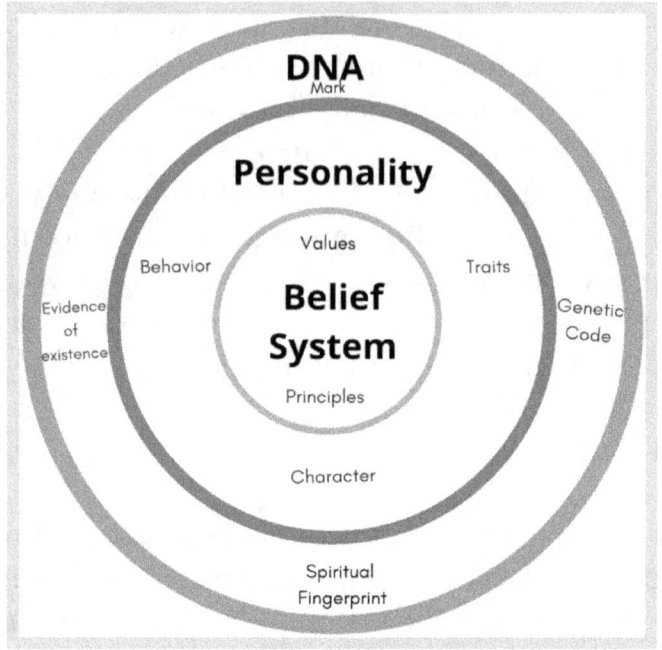

Figure 1

Identity is an internal conviction that leads to a behavior that affirms existence.

If you have children, you understand that when your children are young, they tend to stay close to you. As they get a little older, they will start to explore but they will return to you. This is called the circle of security. They are still dependent on you and circle back to a secure relationship and environment. As they mature into teens, they become more independent and find security in doing things for themselves. However, at this teen stage, they start to look for their own identity. They look to their peers to fit in and for acceptance. This can be a challenge because they are looking for identity, acceptance, and security at the same time.

We seek acceptance because we need validation. When a social group accepts us, we automatically feel validated even though the group may not be good for us. *Instead of seeking greatness, we lower our standards and seek acceptance.* For many young ladies, they bonded with the wrong group. They sought acceptance from individuals and conformed their identity to the group or the individual in order to fit in. From the group that accepts them, they begin the following social group blending process:

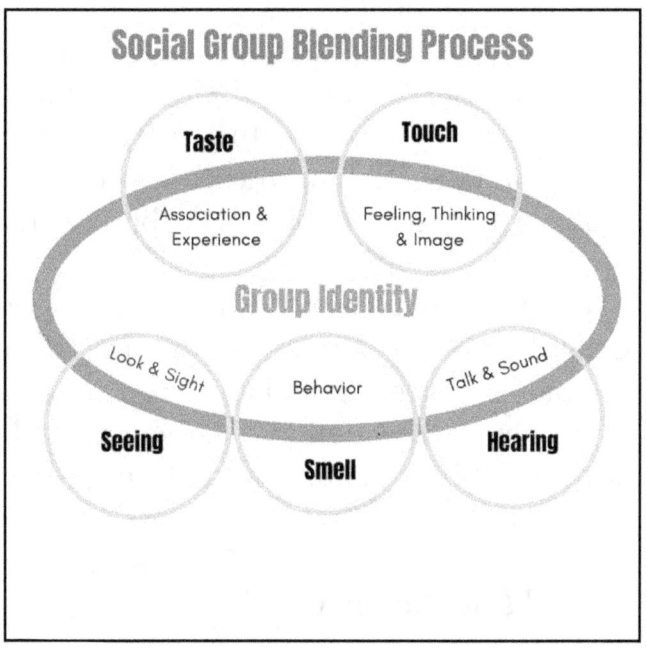

Figure 2

When their senses are engaged they connect and attach.

1. They spend time with them — association and taste (creates an experience)
2. They think like them — image (imagination) touch
3. They talk like them — sound (using the same phrases)
4. They behave like them — smell (speaks of actions)
5. They look like them — sight (may even dress like them)

After this takes place, they look, feel, act, smell, sound and taste like the group that has accepted them. While this may happen at the teenagers' stage, it continues for many of us into adulthood. We seek validation and acceptance from others and we trade our identity for it. We stay in a comfort zone whether the comfort zone is good for us or not. Seeking the comfort of what our group calls normal may not be what is best for us.

Is it possible that the identity we have developed is not ours? Could it be an identity that we pieced together based on our interactions and experiences? How can we find out our true identity? Discovering the nine essential truths about identity can help us answer these questions.

Nine essential truths about identity

1. Identity is formed.

Your identity was formed based on what you were exposed to. *You have learned what to value and this has formed the way you think and process information.* The split-second decisions that you make are filtered through your experiences, what you have learned, and the theories that you have developed over time; these concepts together can produce a reaction in micro seconds.

    2. Identity is a product of repetition.

The things that have happened to you can create a pattern of repetition in your thinking and actions. When we mull over the same thoughts from the past again and again, it creates a mark in our thinking. This mark functions like a bar in music. When a rhythm is repeated over and over again, it produces a behavior pattern. *Repetition is how our subconscious mind functions and navigates us through life; it essentially places us on auto pilot.* When you decide to do something that is not familiar, your conscious mind takes the task from the subconscious mind. Your conscious mind will continue leading until repetition takes over and the subconscious mind can handle it again. Repetition is one of the most effective ways to determine and establish identity.

    3. Behavior is based on your identity.

Behavior is based on your core beliefs. *The things that you identify with identify you.* Culture by itself does not create identity. It is the culture that we accept that affects us. That is why a person can raise two children and they both behave differently. Each child will be affected only by the beliefs they accept. It is those same beliefs that create their behavior and develop their identity.

4. When identity is damaged, broken, or lacking, defensiveness will occur.

If a person is damaged psychologically through abuse or neglect, his or her identity can be deficient. We are like a puzzle. If a piece is missing, we try to fill it with another puzzle piece. Even if the piece is wrong and doesn't fit, we will force another piece into place. *An identity missing validation and acceptance will lack security.* These missing pieces will be replaced with frustration which will lead to defensiveness. Defensiveness is nothing more than an attempt to secure oneself by going into self-protect mode. This mode will lead to contempt, division, and anger along with an incorrect self- image.

5. Identity is tied to purpose.

Who you really are at your core is tied to your purpose. *Purpose is your personal project scope.* To determine your purpose, your identity has to be uncovered and revealed. Uncovering your identity will always give you direction. These two go hand in hand.

6. Not knowing your true identity will cause you to assume someone else's.

Knowing who you are is knowing who you are not. Oftentimes, we see images of people across a screen and they look happy, as if they have everything together.

This is especially true with social media: we look at what people are wearing, what they possess, where they vacation, and their physical attributes. Soon after, we begin to compare ourselves or we try to live up to the standards that are put before us. If we are not careful, we will start seeking the identity in front of us. *It becomes much easier to assume what is before us rather than discover who is within us.*

7. Lost identity creates self-sabotage, which can lead to self-defeating habits.

Self-sabotage is the act of engaging in behavior that is not conducive to growth. Simply put, it involves destructive behaviors to self and others. Not knowing who you are will put you in a wandering and wondering state. Being lost is never fun and can create a fair share of anxiety. When identity is lost and we live from a constant place of anxiety, our needs will go unmet. Unmet needs often lead to addictions, dependence, and self-loathing. *Self-loathing will always lead to self-sabotage.* It is always hard to take good care of the things you hate, including yourself.

8. Knowing identity disciplines your decisions.

Discovering identity will discipline your choices. Understanding your identity will cause your decisions to be focused with an end result in mind. Think of identity like a pastry chef making a chocolate cake. She has her recipe and sticks to it. She makes an outstanding chocolate cake. The cake is in such demand that it is referred to as the "Chocolate Miracle." But if the pastry chef decides to change the ingredients by adding chocolate chips to the ingredients, she would have to rename the new cake because it would no longer be the "Chocolate Miracle." Its identity would be changed. Identity is a **UNIQUE RECIPE**. The decisions that you make affect the recipe and should be in line with who you are and your purpose. This includes your health, financial, emotional, and spiritual decisions.

9. Identity can be changed.

There is good news! Your identity can be changed. To change your identity, it will have to be reformed. To do this, you will have to start at the core, which is your belief system. Remember, your belief system consists of your values, principles, and convictions.

Points to ponder

A. Identity consists of three things: belief system, personality, and DNA.

B. Identity is an internal conviction that leads to a behavior, which affirms existence.

C. Understanding your identity is crucial if you desire to advance and be your most authentic self.

D. Experiences, environments, individuals, and groups can help form identity.

E. Identity is tied to purpose.

Chapter Two

The Exchange

There was a beautiful new cruise vessel docked at the pier. The boat was made for luxury river cruising and could accommodate 100 passengers within its 50 cabins. Due to a worldwide pandemic, the owner of the boat had succumbed to financial hardship, and under that circumstance, the owner of the vessel decided to lease the ship to an import and export firm. The luxury cruise liner would now be used for the transport of goods. The owner believed that she could mitigate her losses through leasing, so the vessel would now be used for short trips to transport goods across the river. The ship did its initial trip and all seemed well. After a few trips, the boat was now carrying fresh produce across the river. The lessee was storing produce in the cabins, as well. New shipments also included tobacco, red wine, alcohol, oil barrels, livestock, and feed.

Sometime after the pandemic was over, the owner decided that she would start doing river cruises again. She arrived early at the dock to see the boat as it was returning from the other side of river with a new shipment. As the ship drew near, it looked just as beautiful as ever. She remembered the first day the new cruise ship was delivered to her at that same dock. She waited patiently as the boat pulled into the dock. Once the boat docked, she boarded the vessel and was horrified by what she saw. The floor was covered with oil spills, feces, and feed! Fruit and vegetable fragments were also seen everywhere! In the cabins, the walls were scratched and were covered with red wine spills and trash! The boat was misused and abused because it was misdirected. She knew that if she wanted to use this ship again for its original intention, it would have to be refurbished.

The same is true for us. When the purpose of a thing is not known, abuse and misuse will follow. Women have often been misunderstood, and being misunderstood, they have often been treated unfairly, abused, and taken advantage of. Women have been made to feel less than through society's unconscious and conscious bias. This has resulted in some women exchanging their experiences for their identity. Once a person's identity is lost, the individual will become lost. At that point, the person will adapt a new identity, perception, and picture of themselves. When the identity of a person changes, so does his/her behavior. Either they will act out of character due to hurt, frustration, and anger or they will accept the status quo while they inwardly harness their emotional pain. The problem will still exist in both scenarios until her identity is restored.

I recently had a conversation with my wife's friend and she shared with me that she was hitting a ceiling spiritually. She went on to say that her interpretation of what God was saying was being filtered by her past experiences. This was obviously causing her deep frustration. After a few moments of silence, she took a deep breath and her next statement described the reason for her feeling this way. She stated, "I feel like I need to replace my dirty filter." This is true for many of us. We look through a mirror or lens that is dim and blurry and we view ourselves not as we actually are. Seeing ourselves this way affects our identity which then affects who we are and what we can accomplish.

Jesus once came across a woman with this same issue. She saw herself the way that others perceived her and not the way God did. She had an identity crisis. She was stuck in how things were and was considered an outcast. She was looking to be loved, honored, and respected but was met with disappointment time and time again. She was looking for something but did not know what. It took a conversation with the King to reveal what she was really searching for and to reveal her true identity. This woman's journey to discovering her true identity starts in the fourth chapter of John.

John 4
¹When therefore the Lord knew how the Pharisees had heard that Jesus made and baptized more disciples than John,

² (Though Jesus himself baptized not, but his disciples,)

³ He left Judaea, and departed again into Galilee.

The scripture said that Jesus was baptizing more disciples than John. The Pharisees were already upset that John was taking some of their followers and Jesus was taking even more. Baptism was not just about being immersed in water; it also represented a school of thought, a teaching. Teaching is one way that our belief system is changed. The Pharisees' school of thought was the Law of Moses, which does not include a relationship with God. They were doing things the way they had always done them and they didn't want to change. They were jealous and envious. Jealousy is a negative emotion. When we act from a negative standpoint, the result will always be negative.

John had gone out into the wilderness and he told the people to repent, for the kingdom of God was near and at hand. That was his school of thought. Jesus' school of thought was the same as John's with an added message that the King, the Messiah, and the Anointed One was finally here. Probably wanting to get away from the Pharisees and their jealousy, He went through a Samarian city called Sycar.

Let's continue reading.

⁴ And he (Jesus) must needs go through Samaria.

⁵ Then cometh he to a city of Samaria, which is called Sychar, near to the parcel of ground that Jacob gave to his son Joseph.

⁶ Now Jacob's well was there. Jesus therefore, being wearied with his journey, sat thus on the well: and it was about the sixth hour.

Samaria was a place that was previously occupied by the Israelites and then conquered by Assyria (2 Kings 23-24). The Assyrian king at that time transported the Israelites out of the land and then moved in many different nations. The people that he moved into the land did not honor God and lions attacked and killed some of them. They realized that something was wrong and asked the king of Assyria for help. The king of Assyria then sent one of Israel's priests back to Samaria to teach the people the customs and about God. So instead of choosing to worship the one true God only, each nation just mixed in the worship of God with the worship of their gods and idols. Their worship was off and this was carried out for many generations. When the Jews moved back to Israel, the people of Samaria continued to occupy that land. The Jews therefore did not want to have anything to do with them because they were not considered Jewish.

Sychar was the place in Samaria where Jacob bought land and dug a well. Hundreds of years later, people were still drinking from it. This proves that the things we do now are going to affect the generations after us. There is a legacy that God has for you. This legacy is great. There is something that He wants you to leave your children, grandchildren, and others. It will supply them with an avenue to have their needs met and be a place that they can drink and feed from for years to come.

Here, we learn about the woman with an identity crisis.

⁷ There cometh a woman of Samaria to draw water: Jesus saith unto her, Give me to drink.

⁸ (For his disciples were gone away unto the city to buy meat.)

⁹ Then saith the woman of Samaria unto him, How is it that thou, being a Jew, askest drink of me, which am a woman of Samaria? for the Jews have no dealings with the Samaritans.

¹⁰ Jesus answered and said unto her, If thou knewest the gift of God, and who it is that saith to thee, Give me to drink; thou wouldest have asked of him, and he would have given thee living water.

¹¹ The woman saith unto him, Sir, thou hast nothing to draw with, and the well is deep: from whence then hast thou that living water?

¹² Art thou greater than our father Jacob, which gave us the well, and drank thereof himself, and his children, and his cattle?

¹³ Jesus answered and said unto her, Whosoever drinketh of this water shall thirst again:

¹⁴ But whosoever drinketh of the water that I shall give him shall never thirst; but the water that I shall give him shall be in him a well of water springing up into everlasting life.

¹⁵ The woman saith unto him, Sir, give me this water, that I thirst not, neither come hither to draw.

¹⁶ Jesus saith unto her, Go, call thy husband, and come hither.

¹⁷ The woman answered and said, I have no husband. Jesus said unto her, Thou hast well said, I have no husband:

¹⁸ For thou hast had five husbands; and he whom thou now hast is not thy husband: in that saidst thou truly.

¹⁹ The woman saith unto him, Sir, I perceive that thou art a prophet.

²⁰ Our fathers worshipped in this mountain; and ye say, that in Jerusalem is the place where men ought to worship.

²¹ Jesus saith unto her, Woman, believe me, the hour cometh, when ye shall neither in this mountain, nor yet at Jerusalem, worship the Father.

²² Ye worship ye know not what: we know what we worship: for salvation is of the Jews.

²³ But the hour cometh, and now is, when the true worshippers shall worship the Father in spirit and in truth: for the Father seeketh such to worship him.

²⁴ God is a Spirit: and they that worship him must worship him in spirit and in truth.

²⁵ The woman saith unto him, I know that Messias cometh, which is called Christ: when he is come, he will tell us all things.

²⁶ Jesus saith unto her, I that speak unto thee am he.

²⁷ And upon this came his disciples, and marvelled that he talked with the woman...

²⁸ The woman then left her waterpot, and went her way into the city, and saith to the men,

²⁹ Come, see a man, which told me all things that ever I did: is not this the Christ?

³⁰ Then they went out of the city, and came unto him.

It was at this well where Jesus had a conversation with a woman who, according to Pharisee practice, was not worthy of His words. His disciples came and saw Him talking with her and wondered why. The Jews didn't even talk with the Samaritans or socialize with them. They were not supposed to go into a home of a Gentile, much less a Samaritan. Recall the time when Peter had a vision as he was praying on a housetop (Acts 10:13-15). Through this vision, the Lord shared with him not to call things that God calls clean, unclean. He further instructed him to go with the men to Cornelius' house, who was a Gentile.

In Matthew 15:6, Jesus said that the traditions of men

make the commands of God of no effect. Mankind has customs that God does not have. This is why John the Baptist's message of repentance and baptism was necessary. Water baptism represents cleaning and refreshing. When we get baptized, it's a symbol of repentance. Repentance is the changing of your mind and behavior. It is an about-face of what we would normally do. John the Baptist was preparing the way by calling for reform in the wilderness, making the crooked places straight. There needed to be a change of how things are viewed and people were qualified. The same is true today. Some may look at you and the things that you have done and disqualify you. God will not because He loves you. He will take the time to talk with you because you are important to Him.

At a time when Jesus should not have been talking to this woman at the well, He decided to have an exchange with her. She was coming to the well to get water and have her thirst quenched. She was driven to the well by a need. Jesus started a conversation with her and said, "Give me a drink." Just think about His opening dialog. Many times, we go to God and we have what we want God to do for us. We are constantly telling God about our needs and wants. "I need this new car" or "I need this bill paid" or "I have this relationship issue" or "I have this problem." We usually come to God with our requests and that is the extent of our prayer. Could it be that we are so self-absorbed that we don't give the Father time to talk? Are we this way because we don't want to hear what He has to say because it might involve us having to do something different? However, at the start of this particular exchange Jesus said "Give me something and serve me."

Points to ponder

A. What is the Lord asking from me?

B. What do I have that I can give to God?

C. During my prayer time do I give the Lord time to share with me?

Chapter Three
Identify

In the previous chapter, we read that Jesus stopped in Sychar, a Samaritan city. Sychar means "a drunken place" or under the influence. Here, He is at a drunken place with people that are mixed in terms of culture and nationality. This Samaritan woman in Sychar comes to the well to satiate. Satiate means to satisfy, to fill, or to indulge in a need. Being under the influence means an altered state of consciousness, attained through ingestion. We have to be careful with what we ingest because what we put inside us will produce actions. The things we ingest can also create an appetite for associate cravings. Just as having sweet sugary snacks can naturally cause you to crave more sweets, the same is true spiritually. What we feed upon mentally and spiritually can cause urges in other areas of our lives.

Identifying Your Thirst

There is a natural thirst and a spiritual thirst.

There are five physical senses and five spiritual senses. These spiritual senses are just as important as the physical senses. Your physical senses communicate to your brain though your body's nervous system. Your spiritual senses communicate with your spiritual heart, which is your core. When your spiritual senses are acute, they bring understanding to your heart. Jesus speaks of seeing and hearing spiritually (Matt 13:15-16). Smell speaks of your actions to include your works, sacrifice, prayers, and behavior (Gen 8:20-21a, Philippians 4:18). Touch has to do with your imagination (Matt 5:28; 2 Corinthians 6:17). You can touch places in your mind without going anywhere physically, so much so that it will send the chemicals to your brain just like you were there physically. Taste speaks of experience (Ps 34:8). When Jesus began to talk to the Samaritan woman about thirst, He addressed her spiritual experience, which is what she had a taste for.

Thirst means a strong desire or longing that is or seems of necessity. It could be a real need or it could seem like a need. We all have thirst. What are you thirsty for? Will it benefit you in the long run or will it bring more hurt than peace? You have to determine whether it's really a need, or if it's something that seems like a need. We can become so impulse-driven that we act from a place of perceived need rather than real need.

Matthew 5:6 says, *"Blessed are they which do hunger and thirst after righteousness: for they shall be filled."* There must be an understanding of thirst, where it comes from, and how it can be addressed so that it does not cause a spiritual disconnect.

The Six Principles of Thirst

1. Thirst comes from a real or perceived need.

You have physical needs and spiritual needs. Physically, you need food, water, and clothing. Spiritually, you need God's Word (Matt 4:4). Just as a tree depends on its connection to the ground, our need to be connected to the Father is the same. You must be honest with yourself and identify your real needs. Your physical senses should not direct you in your determination. Ask God for help in this area.

2. Thirst is the first step of a quest.

Thirst creates a target similar to a place or destination. When a bird is building her nest, she visits different places to gather different sticks and brush for the nest. She is driven by her need to build a nest. Your thirst will drive you to destinations where your potential need can be met. The question we must ask ourselves is are the places and people that we are visiting really helping us accomplish what is good for us? Is it a place that is emotionally or spiritually healthy and helpful?

3. A lack of thirst can cause failure to thrive.

Thirst is like hunger: if you don't have a hunger for anything, you will just sit there and you won't do anything. When the need grows, your motivation to meet that need should grow. Your motivation should cause action. This is what makes you alive. You can usually tell if something is dead or alive by its movement. When you pursue spiritual things, you are alive. However, when you pursue people or things that don't add to you positively, it creates a form of death, which is a failure to thrive.

4. Thirst causes pursuit.

If you went without water for a day or two and there was water at a nearby spring, it would be easy to determine your next move or direction. Your thirst would cause you to pursue what you are thirsty for. That is why it is so important not to be thirsty for the wrong thing. Your pursuit or direction will be off and you will chase things that do not satisfy you.

5. Thirst builds passion.

The thirstier you are for something, the more passionate you become about it. The more you talk about and see it, the more you move towards it. You will have a powerful compelling emotion for the thing that you thirst for. It almost becomes uncontrollable. When passion is directed in the right way, it will link you to your purpose.

6. Thirst will create a method to reach the object of desire.

You will formulate a plan on paper or in your head of how to obtain an objective. This happens for us all of the time and every day on a subconscious level. When the motivation for the thirst is misguided, we become reactionary and conspire rather than plan. Either way, a navigational route of systematic planned behavior will take place to reach the objective.

The Woman at the Well

This woman at the well was thirsty. She was directed by her perceived need. Her thirst was for what was at the source of the well (water), and she came to the source of her desire to get a drink. Jesus explained to her that what she was doing would cause her to be thirsty again. However, He was the Living Water that would satisfy her and she should instead ask Him for a drink. He was having a conversation with her about the water but then again, He was not. He was really saying, "What you've been doing in life isn't going to fulfill you." Jesus wanted her to see what she has been thirsty for had not been the answer. He was saying, "What is your appetite? What is it that is really driving you on the inside?"

After realizing that she was thirsty for more than just natural water, she asked Jesus to give her some of His living water. Jesus replied, "Go get your husband" to which she answered, "I don't have a husband." Jesus countered and told her that in actuality, she had had five husbands and the one she was currently with was not her husband. Imagine this: she married five men, and was living with a sixth. She had a spiritual need, but she was going to the well of the husbands over and over again. Whatever she was trying to get was not there. Jesus told her if you drink from this well, you're going to keep coming back again and again. She knew this was true based on her past, but she kept going back to the man well. Perhaps she thought husband number one didn't love her, so maybe husband number two would? Maybe she thought that husband number three would think that she was beautiful? Maybe she thought that husband four would tell her that he cared for her; perchance husband five was going to stay? Over and over again, she was trying to get her thirst met.

She went back to the men in the city and said, "This guy told me everything I ever did!" Actually, He really didn't. It felt that way to her because He talked to her about what she was thirsty for. Jesus could see into her. She had been trying to quench her thirst - her need - by doing natural things. Her need to feel loved, secure, and beautiful in the eyes of five husbands was not going to be fulfilled by her activity or the action of others. She had a deeper thirst.

Spiritual thirst

What we do naturally is not going to quench the thirst of what we need spiritually. Spiritual needs have to be addressed spiritually. You cannot solve a spiritual problem in the natural because the spiritual realm created the natural realm. Therefore, you should not start in the natural to try to fix things; in fact, you are working backwards. The first thing you need to do is tend to your spiritual need through prayer and then let the Lord lead you in what to do naturally.

This was Israel's biggest challenge. They were constantly trying to meet their needs through other means. Israel would look to other gods for wealth, fertility, agricultural success, and guidance. God delivered Israel from the Egyptians and wanted to place them in the Promised Land. The Promised Land was a place as well as a position. God could have blessed them in the wilderness but He wanted them in position first. He wanted them in a position where he could rain down His blessing on them. It took 40 years in the wilderness for there to be death to the natural way of thinking. After 40 years of being driven by thirst and the natural needs of the flesh, they were finally ready to be put into position in the Promised Land. They were ready to be led by the Spirit, and not by might or by power (Zech 4:6) into the place of favor, blessing, and promise. Yet not long after being in position, they started again looking to other things besides God to meet their needs.

They had a spiritual need for God but did not seek Him. Instead, they looked to have their needs met by doing things their own way. They also sought the other nation's gods for answers. God wanted to be their source and supply. He wanted them to seek Him first (Matt 6:33).

Spiritual Needs Cycle

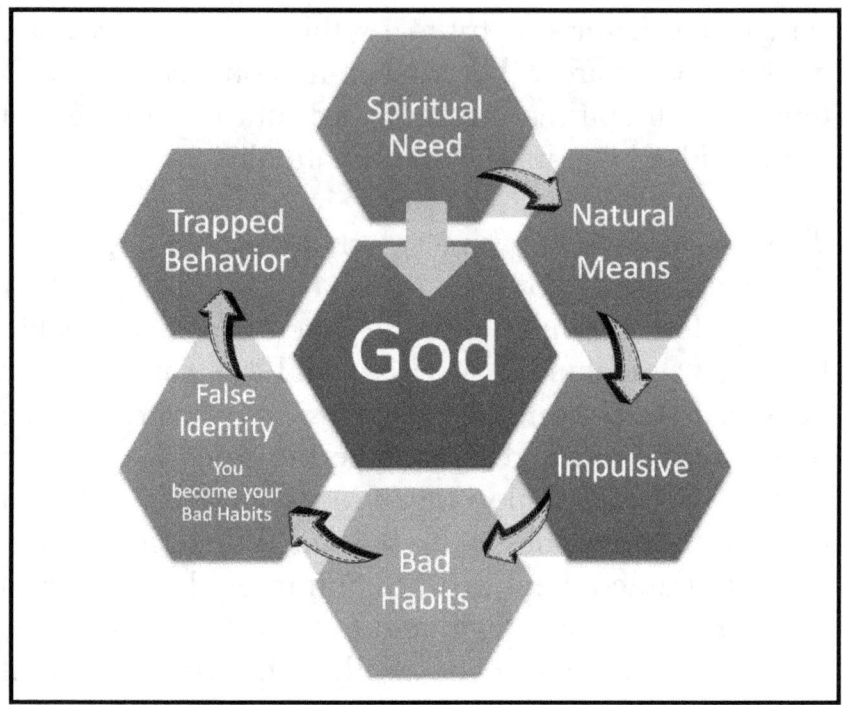

Figure 3

When we attempt to use natural means to fix a spiritual need, we develop impulsive behavior which creates bad habits. This causes us to falsely identify or see ourselves through bad habits and then we end up in a trapped behavior. God calls this trapped behavior, sin. Sin is not God's best for us because sin gives us a false identity. Sin is like the wilderness. God can provide for us there, but it is not the position where He can really pour out His blessing on us. He wants us to look to Him first.

He is the answer and in Him the promises are yes and amen (2 Corinthians 1:20).

People have different definitions of what sin is. Most of the activities we call sin Adam didn't do. We say sleeping around is a sin. Adam didn't do that. Some say smoking cigarettes is a sin. However, I don't think Adam ever smoked cigarettes. Adam and Eve made the mistake and looked to another source to have a need met. They thought they were missing out on something and sought means other than God. This ended in trapped behavior, which is sin. The sin was so great that God had to send Jesus to free mankind from the sin. God wants you to come straight to Him and then He will give you the natural means. He will give you the spiritual impulses. Then you will produce godly habits, and you will begin to identify with Him. This means that you must desire a relationship with God first, and expect your behavior and actions to align as a result.

Let's review the seventeenth chapter of 2 Kings, verses 35 and 36. It says, *"Ye shall not fear other gods, nor bow yourselves to them, nor serve them, nor sacrifice to them: But the LORD, who brought you up out of the land of Egypt with great power and a stretched out arm, him shall ye fear, and him shall ye worship, and to him shall ye do sacrifice."*

When reading this passage, we may say "I don't worship other gods," but a good way to tell what we worship is to think about how and where we spend our time. Another indicator may be how and where we spend our money. We spend time and we spend money. Those are two resources that are important to us.

God says, "Never bow down unto them." He doesn't want you submitted under anything. You were designed to have dominion and power; to tread upon the enemy, serpents, and everything that the devil has (Luke 10:19). God says never serve them. Do not follow them, obey them, or become their servant. Never sacrifice to them, do not give to them, or offer up to them. He wants us to seek His face. *What we behold, we become.* His desire is for us to come to Him, to behold Him, and we will become like Him.

Points to ponder

A. Have I been seeking natural things first?

B. What has my thirst cause me to pursue?

C. How do I get from a wilderness mentality to a Promised Land mentality?

Chapter Four
Inquest

Think back to the conversation that I had with my wife's friend in which she stated, "I feel like I need to replace my dirty filter." In order for her to have come to this conclusion, she had to do some introspection. This is the identifying stage. The woman at the well had to do some introspection, too. This meeting with Jesus caused questions to arise within her. She did not realize that the questions at the well would lead to the same questions she would later have to ask herself. While the questions started off from a natural perspective, they would later expand into spiritual questions. I call these "the well questions."

"Well" Questions

Why

Jesus' request for a drink was met with her saying, "**Why** are you asking me for a drink?" Her thinking behind this was that the Jews didn't communicate with Samaritans. She had a hard time getting past her cultural differences. Culture can give us a position naturally because we have others that we can relate with. They often think and believe the same things that we do because of our exposure and experience. It becomes a stance that we can rely on and it gives us importance. Culture is important, but we should never allow our cultural differences or similarities to hold us back.

What/How

Jesus explained to her that if she knew the gift that God had for her, she would ask Him for living water. Her next question was, "**What** are you going to draw with?" In other words, how was this going to be done? Her experience from her many visits to the well was that it was deep. She knew that in order to have her need met, He needed a device or means to carry out the task. When she looked at Jesus, she didn't see anything that He could use. She was looking at what He had in his physical possession. Meanwhile, Jesus had taken inventory of her soul and the thirst that was driving her. He saw that there was a deep need inside of her and that need had to be addressed in order for her to thrive.

Where
It dawned on her that Jesus was not talking about natural water or a source, but living water. Then she asked, "**Where** is this water coming from? I don't see it." She was thinking naturally. Where also speaks of destination. You can determine the resources you will need, but don't worry about where they are going to come from. Worry detracts while faith attracts. In Matthew 6, Jesus instructed us to not have anxiety about resources, to include food, clothing, water, etc. He went on to say that our Heavenly Father knows that we have need of these things. Then He shared with us a major life lesson on priorities: that we should seek first the kingdom of God and His righteousness and all of these things (resources) will be attracted or added to us. When God gives us the vision for where He wants us to go, He will also give us the provision when we seek Him and His right ways. Don't stress about where things are going to come from. Instead, seek your Heavenly Father who knows your needs and will supply them. Let your faith supersede any worry.

Where also speaks of location, not just in terms of where you would like to end up, but also your current location. Knowing your current location is just as important as knowing your destination. Where are you mentally, emotionally, spiritually and yes, physically? Are you at an address emotionally that you should have left years ago? Being real with yourself about where you are in life takes courage. In Gen 3:8-10 after Adam ate the fruit and God came looking for him, Adam went and hid himself behind the trees. God called for him saying, "Where are you?" After seeking his own provision, he became afraid of the presence of God and went into hiding; he hid himself emotionally, spiritually and physically. This is not the address where God wants you to live. He has a better place for you. He has a vision for you to take you into a place of promise where He can prosper you. Where do you see yourself? Where is your new God destination? What is your end result? Without having a picture of your new address, you will not know when you have arrived.

Who

As she continued to process what was actually taking place, she went back to her cultural thinking. She basically asked Jesus, "**Who** are you? Are you greater than Jacob, our father Jacob?" She finally arrived at identity, but with a comparison to her past understanding from teachings about Jacob. What is interesting about the reference to Jacob is that she and the village identified with Jacob rather than his name change. After Jacob wrestled with the angel, he was renamed Israel, which means "Prince of God." She identified him as who he was, not who he had become. This cultural identification was probably causing her to see dimly and blurry as to who God was saying she was. She was not her history or the sum of her experiences!

These were powerful questions that this woman asked at the well. They are equally powerful when we internalize them and ask ourselves these same life questions.

Why?
"Why" has to do with your purpose. Why am I here? What is your reason for existing?
We all have a purpose and a reason for being here on earth at this time. Your purpose will usually not just benefit you, but others, too. Determining your gifts and talents can also point you in the direction of your purpose. What are you good at? What do you enjoy doing? What do you hate? These are just some things to consider when discovering your purpose.

What? and **How** is the **what** going to happen?
Identify what needs to be done. How are you going to accomplish it? This requires you to develop a plan of action. What are the natural sequential ordered steps toward completing your goal?

Where?
Determine the resources needed. Don't worry about where they are going to come from. When God gives the vision, He will give the provision. Where also determines your destination. Where is your end result? How will you know that you've accomplished it?

Who?
Who are you? Know your identity, strengths, and weaknesses. Reflect and ask God to introduce you to the real you. How can you use your uniqueness and differences to affect change? This question has to do

with identity. When this question is answered, our identity and character are defined. This sobering question can assist us in locating ourselves as we become balanced and in control.

People have defined us by our own actions, their actions, and what we have permitted or allowed to take place in our lives. Our self-assessment should not be shaped by the opinions of others who offer these opinions without any substance. We have to untangle ourselves from the web of people-pleasing to really discover who we are at the core. This can become frightening because we often see our negative parts as greater than our positive attributes. When you dig, you may find gold but you may also find dirt and unwanted things. This is good because this helps you build true character. Everything about us is not always pleasant, but to get to the good stuff we have to often plow through the dirt. Gold, diamonds, and precious stones are not usually on the surface; typically you have to dig for them.

Who was this woman at the well? What was her true story? What did she really endure at the hands of others? Was she happy playing a role that had been laid out for her? Did she have a dream that was crushed by her environment? Was she just a sexual toy, a punching bag, or a servant sent to get water? Was she a victim? Did they label her as stupid, useless, or foolish? Did she wrestle with her emotions as she felt one thing within her but saw something completely different in the people around her? Was she the sum of her experiences or was her experience just a part of her story? How could she separate her experiences from her identity?

Who are you? The same questions apply, but don't ask anyone else. Ask the Lord. The same Lord that took His time to talk to this woman at the well, whom society would say was worthless, also wants to take His time and talk to you. The creator of all things knows your purpose. Ask the Creator, God, "Who am I?" Your identity comes from Him.

When we can answer these life questions with clarity and certainty, we will walk in our path of greatness. This all starts when we hear Jesus say, "Give me to drink," or "Serve me." Once we accept our position to serve, greatness is released. Your purpose is wrapped in your service.

Jeff Bezos, the founder of Amazon, decided to serve people with an option to purchase books online. He knew that he wanted to sell everything from A to Z on the internet, but he needed a starting point. His starting point was books and then he slowly added new areas until he now serves the world with his gift, which is providing people the opportunity to purchase everything from A to Z. This was no accident. He had to answer these same questions in order to reach his quest. Answering these life questions will give you direction, hope, and a future.

Points to ponder

A. What are your dreams?

B. When you close your eyes what do you see? Be honest

C. What do you want to see?

D. Are you defined by your experiences or by what God says about you?

Chapter Five

Attachment

Everything you do has a corresponding action. In Physics, Newton says that whenever you push against something, there is a force pushing back at you, which is called resistance. If I push my son's toy car across the kitchen floor, it pushes back with a force. I don't feel it because I am applying more force than the toy car has. On the other hand, when I go outside and try to push my car, I can immediately feel the car pushing back at me with force. When I use a greater force than the car, the car will move. Spiritual force is the same. For progress to be made spiritually, we need to use a greater force than our opposition.

There will be resistance in anything you try to do, but don't think that just because there is resistance that you need to stop. There are things that you have been struggling with and God wants to help remove the struggle. God is power and there is nothing greater than His force. When we are on His side, things have to move out of the way. Our struggles that we face repeatedly have everything to do with our needs that go unmet. The forces that are working against us move us because we have not quenched our thirst by seeking God in that area. This is clearly seen after the woman asks for this living water from Jesus. His response was, "Go get your husband" but He was really saying, "Go get me the thing you are thirsty for. Go bring him to me. Bring the thing that you have been filling up on, the thing that you've tried to use to quench your thirst."

It is time to say goodbye to the thing that you have been fighting with over and over. It doesn't matter how long it's been in your family or genealogy. You might be surprised if you knew that you are dealing with the same thing that your grandmother went through. Remember that Jacob dug the well and it affected future generations. There may have been some things that were dug up by grandma, great-grandma, and so on that were negative. These things could have affected you too, and your identity. It is time to put an end to this. Simply put, you have to bring your driving thirst—the unmet need—to Jesus. He can't give you living water until you bring it to Him. There has to be a sacrifice and an exchange on your part. When you bring <u>your need</u> to Him <u>and the thing that you have used to fill that need</u>, you join forces with Him. Then He will satisfy your need and give you life.

Don't have the same response as the woman at the well initially had when Jesus told her to, "Go get your husband." She checked out on Jesus and began to make an excuse. She stated, "I don't have a husband" as she was trying to hide her need. Jesus replied, "True, he is not your husband and you have had five others". He was pointing out that no one and no object had been able to meet her need. She had a deep need to be loved. The gift of God was sitting there on the well letting her know that she was acceptable in His eyes. He wanted her to recognize her adverse attachment and bring it to him.

Getting Rid of Issues
Hiding or exposing the attachment

As we go through life, there are many things that we can get attached to. There are also many things that try to attach to us. There are some things that we do that cause associate attachments to come looking for us.

There is a synergistic element attached to our feelings and desires. For instance, if I choose to dwell negatively about something that my spouse did, it will not be long before I am thinking about other times when she annoyed me, which are associate attachments. Eventually, I will come to a place where that's all I will see about her. If this goes unchecked, then I will only see her negatively and everything that she does will annoy me.

Our feelings bring companion feelings and our thoughts bring companion thoughts. Spirits bring companion spirits. This is why Jesus said many times after someone was delivered to go and sin no more. He didn't want them to return to the same behavior and the same circumstance.

Just because things have attached themselves to you does not mean that you did something wrong or that a spirit is involved, but the presence of an issue is the presence of *something*. That is why something of greater force has to remove or subdue it. When Jesus was in a boat and the sea was roaring and the wind was blasting, He was able to displace the storm by a stronger force (Mark 4:35-40). When Jesus landed at the seashore, a man with an unclean spirit met Him and Jesus commanded the unclean spirit to leave. Whether it is a spirit or not, a stronger power has to displace it. This is the way deliverance works. It displaces issues, spirits, disease, and brokenness, and makes things whole or well so that we can experience freedom.

In Mark 5:25-29, there is an example of a woman who went through some challenges and had some issues.

We have no record that she did anything wrong or that a spirit was involved, but we do know that she had an issue.

The text reads:

25 And a certain woman, which had an issue of blood twelve years,

26 And had suffered many things of many physicians, and had spent all that she had, and was nothing bettered, but rather grew worse,

27 When she had heard of Jesus, came in the press behind, and touched his garment.

28 For she said, If I may touch but his clothes, I shall be whole.

29 And straightway the fountain of her blood was dried up; and she felt in her body that she was healed of that plague.

30 And Jesus, immediately knowing in himself that virtue had gone out of him, turned him about in the press, and said, Who touched my clothes?

31 And his disciples said unto him, Thou seest the multitude thronging thee, and sayest thou, Who touched me?

32 And he looked round about to see her that had done this thing.

33 But the woman fearing and trembling, knowing what was done in her, came and fell down before him, and told him all the truth.

34 And he said unto her, Daughter, thy faith hath made thee whole; go in peace, and be whole of thy plague.

This woman had an issue, and she spent all that she had. She was literally and figuratively spent! When we have an issue, we spend time, money, and resources to figure a way out. This happens often. We start running around and doing a lot of natural things and lose our focus. Many times, we hide our issues from everyone. We may even try to hide it from God, but He knows, so there is no sense in being false. Bring it to Him, to the One who can liberate you. Be open, honest with Him and yourself.

Four reasons why we hide our issues

1. Our issues make us seem weak and we don't want to seem weak to others or ourselves. The truth is that everyone has issues or trials that they go through. Admitting that we have an issue doesn't make us weak, but tolerating an issue does.

2. We become attached to them. We don't want to let the issue go. It may not be good for us but there is a level of familiarity. Maybe it has been 12 years or more and we have made accommodations for it. Rather than reject it, we just accepted it.

3. We begin to identify with the issue more than with God. This is when our issue is wrapped up with our identity. In this instance, losing our issue is like losing our identity. Losing the issue feels

like grieving the death of self in some way or form. It just seems better to hold on to the issue rather than releasing it.

4. We just like our issue/issues. We cuddle up with the issue. It makes us feel good. We enjoy it and it brings us security and pleasure.

Points to ponder

A. Are there things that you have an attachment to?

B. Why do you think you have this attachment?

C. What do you fear about letting this attachment go?

Chapter Six
Un-Wrap

The woman with the issue of blood in the book of Mark made the decision to go to Jesus with her issue. From that decision, she went from being called the woman with the issue to "Daughter" (v34). Jesus called her, "Daughter." *You are God's Daughter!* When we bring our issue to Him, an exchange takes place, but you have to decide that enough is enough and that you are going to take your issues to Jesus. Mark 5:28 gives us insight into her faith: "For she said if I may but touch his clothes I shall be whole." When we take our issues to Him, He exchanges our issues and gives us a touch, an encounter that wraps us in His grace. *When we unwrap our association with the issue, He wraps us in grace.* Then what we could not do in our natural strength becomes easier with His grace. His grace is not just unmerited favor, but His power, force, and ability working through us.

She stopped spending money, time, and efforts on natural things. She was spent and had no money; she was broke. She went to all of the doctors, and no one could help her. She was in a hopeless state. Then after hearing about Jesus and what he could do, she began to spend her efforts, to include her time and reasoning, on reaching Him for a touch and to have an encounter. She said within herself, "If I can touch his garment, I will be made whole." Her faith spoke. It was that one statement that got her healed. She was healed from that statement before she got there and touched Him. She touched Him spiritually before she touched Him naturally. When she went to do the natural thing, which was to touch Him, what she had spoken into existence had already spiritually taken place. She made Jesus her priority. She took her issue to Jesus, the Christ (the

Anointed One). Jesus was the One who could do something about it and an exchange took place. Her issue left and she was made well.

My Issue

When I began to search for gold in my personal life in order to find out who I really was, I came across some things that were buried deep in the dirt. There were many things, but I will share this one;

My mindset about food was an issue. This affected my self-esteem and identity. It's an issue that I had since I was a child, and I knew that I had to get a grip on this thing that had been holding me back. I was using self-defeating habits that were not productive for my health. I needed to start taking care of my body, because I realized that if I didn't take care of my body and my body dies, my spirit would be expelled. It doesn't matter how strong my spirit is. When the body dies, the spirit leaves. My body is the temple of God and I have to take care of it.

God started dealing with me with taking care of my body. Let me just be transparent: I have lost a lot of weight at different times in my life only to gain it back in one to three years. The experience has been like a yo-yo: up and down. I said to my wife, "I have to do something extreme to lose the weight." Extreme works for me. I go overboard. I get that from my dad. I was not sure what I needed to do but I asked the Lord for help, and I decided to take my issue to Him.

As God would have it, I ran into an old friend that I

used to see at the gym. We greeted each other and I said, "Man, you look good, what's going on? What are you doing?" He shared with me that he was fasting two days a week. I knew there was a spiritual benefit to fasting but I didn't know there was a natural benefit to it. I decided to pray about it and study it from the Bible's perspective. I was looking for a natural result but I was going to put the spiritual first. I was led to fast for four days. After that four day fast, I was lit. I know that is a slang word today, but that's the only way I can describe how I felt: I was lit. I didn't even care if I ate; I wanted to be in the presence of God. I wanted to feel that way all of the time. I felt clean inside, and I felt like I was hearing from God so well.

I came off the fast and then started to fast twice a week on Tuesdays and Thursdays. I was not only doing the fast naturally but I was reading my Bible and praying more in order to maintain what my spirit needed. I woke up on one fast day and realized that I didn't have time to pray. I am a minister and believe it or not, that happens to us, too. I started running around with issues: Kids to camp, doing this, doing that, and then I came back home. I said to my wife, "Today I have been fasting but for some reason I feel hungry. Why do I feel hungry today?" I didn't usually feel hungry when I was fasting. I told her that I was going to go downstairs and spend some time with the Lord. I went in my prayer room, I closed the door, and I was in there for an hour and a half. I came back out and I was not hungry at all; I felt full. I thought, "How many times had I thought that I was hungry naturally when I really needed spiritual food/drink?" The feeling of spiritual hunger and physical hunger can feel the same. Maybe you have been feeling a certain way physically because you are feeling that way spiritually. There could be a spiritual hunger/thirst that you are experiencing that is directly related to a spiritual deficit.

This was the case with the woman at the well. She was looking for some form or fashion of security and validation. I don't know if her father left her, if she had issues with her mother, or if she was abandoned or something else. I do know that she had settled in a location (environment) that had a reputation for being a drunken place (under the influence). Perhaps you have settled for a place and have identified with your environment. You may even have a false sense of security. Could it be that you have an empty space spiritually and you have tried to fill that empty space with food, TV, drugs, alcohol, work, or family, which are all natural things? Maybe you don't like to be alone or when you are alone you must have noise. Is this so you don't have to hear the empty space call to you? Whatever the issue is, more than likely it is affecting your identity.

If a person's mind is filled with issues from unmet needs this will cause the person to see a picture of him/herself as inadequate and not good enough. Strip away the façade, mask, and defensiveness that you have covered yourself with in an effort to self-protect. Self-reflection is the key. *The right perception clears the way for having the right perspective.* This is why identifying the issues internally will help you in discovering your true identity. Seeing clearly who you are will aid in you seeing who you are not.

In Luke 15:11-18, there is the story of a son who was having an identity crisis. He decided to ask his father (while he was alive) for his share of his inheritance. The father gave both of his sons their inheritance and after a few days, the young son left his father's home. Leaving home demonstrated that he was leaving his circle of security. He ended up wasting all of his inheritance in a far country and then found himself broke. More bad news followed with there being a famine in the land. His next action was to join himself with a citizen of that country, which meant that he was thinking, acting, looking, speaking and feeling like the people he surrounded himself with. He then became defined as a servant, which signaled an identity change, and he had to go feed the hogs. He became so hungry, physically and spiritually, that he would have eaten the hogs' food. But his hunger had an interesting effect: *it caused him to self-reflect and come to himself.* His identity began to take a shift and he began to speak to himself in faith by saying, "How many hired servants of my father's have bread enough to spare, and I perish with hunger? I will arise and go to my father".

After this identity shift, he went home to his father with the mindset that he would be a servant for him. He was suffering from a lost identity, not sure about who he really was. In this state, he was willing to accept another's identity. As he was on his way back to his father's house, his father saw him from afar and ran to greet him. The prodigal began to talk to his father about the new servant identity that he would embody, but his father ignored his recital and commanded that the servants clothe him in the best robe, put a ring on his hand, and place shoes on his feet. He also commanded that they prepare the fatted calf and celebrate because his son who was lost was now home. It took the son to come to the father to be restored to his true place and identity. He had to see himself like the father saw him in order to enjoy the experiences of a son.

Maybe you have some misguided thinking about who you are supposed to be or even how you think the Father is supposed to see you. When you come to Him with that lower-level talk, He ignores that discourse. Instead, He greets you and says, "Welcome home, Daughter!" There is a robe, ring and some shoes waiting for you. The Father is ready to celebrate you! He has been waiting for you to come to yourself and to come to Him so He could reestablish you with the correct image, identity, and experience.

Live in a way that causes you to be authentic to the Father and yourself. This will cause you to live your best life. You have something that will fulfill you only when you accomplish it as it is your purpose. You won't be able to accomplish your purpose until you become real with yourself. There is so much at stake and you deserve to live a life that fulfils you and compliments your true self.

See yourself, agree with yourself, and be yourself!

Allen Forbes
www.afspeaks.com

Points to Ponder

A. Can you identify any self-defeating habits in your life?

B. Un-wrapping your association with the issue wraps you in God's grace.

C. What/who do you look for to feel secure?

D. What is your environment like and what do you need to change about it?

E. Self-reflection is needed to have the right perception and for having the right perspective.

The Conclusion

Meet Him at your well!

Matthew 6:33
³⁵But seek ye first the kingdom of God, and his righteousness; and all these things shall be added unto you.

God wants to help you with your issues but you have to bring them to Him in prayer. The following is a prayer that you can pray to start the conversation with the Father. Read through it first, and then pray it after you are sure what you want to say. The Father is at the well waiting to commune with you. Just start the tough conversation and allow Him to tell you who you really are and what to do. Seek Him first and allow Him to lead you into what you should do naturally.

Prayer

Father, I bless you. You are worthy, you are awesome. There is none like You. You are the most powerful and awesome God, the Creator of Heaven and Earth. I magnify You, and make You bigger and larger than any issue that I am facing. I ask today for that living water that will cause me not to thirst after the wrong things. Show me what I am really thirsty and hungry for and what is at the root of my issues. I invite you into my _____ (issue). I want to give up trying to solve that issue myself and with natural means only.

May all generational curses be broken and the generational blessings proceed forward with me and the generations after me. Every issue that I have fought with and struggled with, I bring it to You. I lay it at Your feet in exchange for a touch from You. I pray for Your grace and empowerment to conquer what has tried to conquer me. I declare that Your anointing is released now over my life to set me free. Show me what to do spiritually and naturally as I walk in this newfound liberation. Lead me each day that I will not fall into the trap of the enemy. Direct my steps to a place of safety and peace. Show me who I really am and how I should view myself as Your daughter. Surround me with people who love me, see me, and care for me. Remove those from my path that are jealous and harmful. Let my true identity be exposed as Your light shines through me. Thank You for seeing and hearing me. Thank You for restoration, healing of past hurts, and mental and emotional balance. Thank You for courage and the perseverance in my transformational journey to discovering my true identity. May I be perfected in Your presence!

God bless you on your journey!

If you enjoyed reading this book, please leave a favorable review on Amazon.com

Introduction to the King

Maybe by some off chance you picked up this book and you have never met the King. I would like to take this time to introduce you to Him. He came, died and bled for you because He loves you. His name is Jesus and He longs to have a relationship with you. In order to have this relationship with Him you will have to invite Him to come and live in your heart. You can do this by praying and inviting Him in. If you would like to do so, please read the prayer below and then pray it to Him with sincerity.

Prayer
God I am a sinner and I believe that Jesus died for the forgiveness of my sin. I believe that Jesus Christ was raised from the dead and is my Lord and Savior. You loved me so much that you gave your Son so I could be a part of your family. I invite You to come and live in my heart. Please lead and guide me as my new Lord in the kingdom of God.

It is that simple (Romans 10:9). If you prayed and believe this prayer please reach out to us so we can connect with you. In the meantime, find a good bible believing church that you can become a part of.

Continue to read the bible to discover your true identity.

Welcome to the Kingdom! Enjoy getting to know the King.

Reach out to us at www.LivingLifeInt.org

About the Author

Allen Forbes is a Christian author and speaker who is dedicated to encouraging others to recognize and pursue their identity in God. He is a licensed minister, with a background of 20+ years of faithful serving and stewardship in ministry. Allen has spent decades in the business arena in roles that included service, management, sales, and entrepreneurship. He is the co-founder of Living Life International a faith-based nonprofit that inspires, educates and informs. You will find a combination of biblical principles, humor and extensive business wisdom in his books and presentations. Originally from Brooklyn, NY Allen and his family reside in Maryland.

Connect with Allen through social media

www.facebook.com/AuthoringInspiration

www.instagram.com/allen.forbes.12

Other Books

www.AFspeaks.com

Sandbox Personalities Book

Kingdom Dynamics Book

www.ingramcontent.com/pod-product-compliance
Lightning Source LLC
LaVergne TN
LVHW051527070426
835507LV00023B/3351